MANAGING HOUSING CONTRACTS:
A GOOD PRACTICE GUIDE

ANNE KING AND JOHN NEWBURY

CHARTERED INSTITUTE OF HOUSING

The Chartered Institute of Housing
The Chartered Institute of Housing is the professional organisation for all people who work in housing. Its purpose is to take a strategic and leading role in encouraging and promoting the provision of good quality affordable housing for all. The Institute has more than 13,000 members working in local authorities, housing associations, the private sector and educational institutions.

Chartered Institute of Housing
Octavia House, Westwood Way
Coventry CV4 8JP
Telephone: 01203 694433

Managing Housing Contracts: A Good Practice Guide
Written by Anne King and John Newbury

Legal advice in the preparation of this Guide has been provided by Ian Doolittle of Trowers & Hamlins, Solicitors

Commissioning Editor: Ross Fraser

© Chartered Institute of Housing 1996
Published by the Chartered Institute of Housing

ISBN 0 901607 93 2

Graphic design by Jeremy Spencer
Printed by Genesis Print & Marketing

Whilst all reasonable care and attention has been taken in compiling this publication, the authors, the publishers and the legal adviser regret that they cannot assume responsibility for any error or omission that it contains. Readers should take legal, financial and other appropriate advice before taking specific action in relation to this subject.

All rights reserved. No part of this publication may be reproduced, stored in a retrieval system or transmitted in any form or by any means, electronic, mechanical, photocopying, recording, or otherwise without the prior permission of the publishers.

Contents

ABOUT THE AUTHORS

Anne King and John Newbury are Directors of Newbury King Consultants. They have been closely involved throughout the current round of housing management compulsory competitive tendering (HMCCT) and since 1992 have personally worked on the majority of voluntary delegations of housing management (i.e. tendering without an in-house bid) and Department of the Environment and Scottish Office HMCCT pilot studies.

Newbury King Consultants is currently working with local housing authorities to help ensure that real and lasting benefits are secured for tenants and leaseholders despite the distraction and disruption caused by HMCCT. It is also working with housing associations in order that their tenants can benefit from that experience as well without enduring the uncertainties of competitive tendering. In the wide range of management consultancy work that Newbury King Consultants undertakes with housing service providers, a key theme has been highlighted by HMCCT. That is, that both those responsible for actual service delivery and their customers have for too long suffered from ill-defined service levels and extravagant policy commitments. The emergence of a tendered specification and a commissioning client role provides an opportunity and a focus of responsibility for supporting the housing managers while ensuring that tenants and leaseholders get the published level of service. Anne King and John Newbury have, therefore, maintained as a theme of this Guide that it is good practice for the HMCCT client to develop a continuing role and constructive relationship with the successful service provider **whoever** it turns out to be.

Newbury King Consultants exists to provide strategic advice and practical assistance to a wide range of public service providers, their associations and suppliers, and to government departments and agencies. This brings experience of tendering, market testing and purchaser provider relationships in other service sectors to help inform good practice guidance for the emerging housing management client role.

ACKNOWLEDGEMENTS

This Guide is based on our work with a wide range of client and contractor organisations and we wish to acknowledge their contribution to its development.

Particular thanks are due to officers of the following local authorities who gave their time and helpful comments during the drafting of the Guide:
   Dartford Borough Council
   East Hertfordshire District Council
   London Borough of Brent
   London Borough of Richmond upon Thames
   Oxford City Council.

Thanks are also due to Ian Doolittle of Trowers & Hamlins, Solicitors for checking the legal accuracy of the text. Ian Doolittle is the author of the ADC/AMA *Model Form of Contract for Housing Management Services*.

Newbury King & Co. Ltd.
Management Consultants
Hereford House
23/24 Smithfield Street
London EC1A 9LB
Telephone: 0171-329 1919

CHAPTER 1

INTRODUCTION

❏ Use of terms

Most of the guidance given in this publication is equally relevant whether a housing management contract has been awarded to an in-house or external contractor. Strictly speaking, a local authority cannot enter into a legally binding contract with itself, but for clarity the following terms have the meanings shown.

Terms	Meanings
Client	The person or team commissioning the services delivered under the contract and therefore responsible for its management.
(Housing management) Contractor	The service provider under the contract – being either the directly employed service organisation (DSO) or an external body.
Contract	The agreement between the client and contractor based on the bid price and contract documentation.
Customers	Tenants and leaseholders as users of the landlord services provided under the contract.

A glossary of other terms used in the Guide can be found at Appendix C.

❏ Background to this Good Practice Guide

The compulsory competitive tendering of public sector services has been around since the Local Government Planning and Land Act 1980. However, the nature of a housing service within the context of the 'white collar' round of Local Government Act 1988 compulsory competitive tendering (CCT) breaks new ground. Housing management is a service that affects the lives of a significant proportion of the population all day, every day. Equally important, it is a service with only a limited number of visible and quantifiable outputs. The remainder of the required service outcomes have generally been described in local authority service plans and policies in the terms of customer care, value for money, equality of access and treatment and pursuit of quality. Customers know when their dustbin has not been emptied, can prove the point and expect the local authority to enforce the service specification; but how do they know if they have received the specified level of value, quality and equality in housing management?

Two things of relevance to this Good Practice Guide have arisen from this dilemma.

First, and to their credit, most local authorities have succeeded in specifying the inputs, outputs and processes which add up to their required service outcomes. In fact many, and perhaps most, would acknowledge that whilst CCT has distracted them from concentrating on service delivery, they do recognise the value of a specification in **planning** services and **managing** performance to meet documented customer and councillor expectations.

Second, because of the workload and the uncertainties of CCT, both the client and direct services organisation (DSO) have tended not to look further ahead than the award of a contract. Even where authorities planned their contract monitoring arrangements at an early stage, there was often an unwillingness to discuss life beyond the contract award. In fact, with some notable exceptions, the early monitoring models appear to have been developed to give a 'warning' to the external competition of likely difficulties in running the contracts. They have counter-productively submerged both client and contractor in bureaucracy when piloted with the DSO during 'dummy runs' for CCT.

Consequently, most attention has focused on the competition legislation and the performance of the DSO as a prospective in-house contractor. Less thought has been given to the role and expected performance of the client. How many staff are required to do what? How will the contract be managed rather than simply monitored? What are the roles of customers and the contractor in providing monitoring information?

The primary argument advanced in this Guide is simple. If the contract fails to deliver, or (worse still) is terminated, the client will be at least partly responsible and wholly accountable for the failure.

❏ What this Guide is about

The Guide deals with **contract management** which comprises two distinct but linked client activities:

- **contract monitoring** which is the basis of an assessment of whether the service has been delivered as specified; and

- **contract administration** which is the management of the relationship with the contractor including meetings, payment, contract variation and the default procedure.

The effectiveness of both contract monitoring and contract administration depends to a significant extent on the clarity and enforceability of the specification and conditions of contract. These in turn should reflect a consistent tendering strategy. Therefore, contract management and the role and operating cost of the client function should have been taken into account when drawing up the tender documentation. A *Model Form of Contract for Housing Management Services* has been published by the Association of District Councils and the Association of Metropolitan Authorities and authorities are strongly recommended to refer to it when drawing up their own documentation. This Guide cannot fully overcome any inadequacy in the tender documentation. It will, however, assist in making best use of the existing contractual relationship for those authorities that have let contracts and it is never too late to implement good practice. It will also help authorities in the preliminary stages of tendering to take account of contract management in their strategies and documentation.

❏ Who is the Guide for?

This Guide is designed to help the client to maintain and improve service delivery after the award of a contract under compulsory competitive tendering of housing management.

The underlying assumption is that the primary objective of the client is to deliver high quality services that represent good value for money. Quality in this context is taken to mean the meeting of customer requirements as reflected in the service specification. The Guide makes it clear that the principles of contract management apply whether the contract is awarded in-house or to an external tenderer. The practical application of those principles may be different in those two circumstances but the objectives remain the same.

The Guide is aimed primarily at local authority client officers because they are the accountable commissioners of the service and will also be responsible for advising and assisting councillors and customers.

❏ National variations in Scotland, Wales and England

The CCT timetables for Scotland, Wales and England vary because of the different local government reorganisation timetables in Wales and Scotland. However, once implemented, the principles of contract management for housing management CCT are the same.

A significant legislative difference is that the tenant consultation provisions of the Leasehold Reform, Housing and Urban Development Act 1993 apply only in England and Wales. However, Scottish Office guidance in Circular 20/1995 *Housing Management Compulsory Competitive Tendering: Arrangements for Tenant Involvement and Consultation* largely replicates existing Department of the Environment guidance to authorities in England and Wales.

❏ Delegation of responsibility

The first housing management contracts to be let were called voluntary delegation of management (VDM). This was in order to distinguish these early exercises, which did not include an in-house bid, from voluntary competitive tendering (VCT) and compulsory competitive tendering (CCT) which are subject to statutory regulation under the Local Government Act 1988. However, regardless of the terminology and despite the element of compulsion, all tendering has the objective of **delegation of responsibility** for delivering the services for which the client remains **accountable**.

In other words, the client meets its accountability for service delivery through a single contract rather than through a number of individual contracts of employment and a chain of delegations. Accordingly, all the management principles of delegation apply to the tendering strategy and to effective contract management.

Delegation is a process not a one-off activity and it involves a positive and continuing relationship between the delegater and delegatee; in this case the client and contractor respectively. For the delegation to achieve its key objectives of delivering the specification to the contract standard:

- **the client should:**
  - 'let go' of operational matters but with periodic review;
  - be available for advice and discussion;
  - provide training on client administrative and computer systems, particularly for an external contractor;
  - allow for a learning process and corrective action by both the client and contractor;
  - delegate authority to match responsibility, e.g. for client-agent role of the contractor;
  - provide information relevant to the task; and
  - give timely feedback to enhance the chances of success of the delegation.
- **the client should not:**
  - interfere in operational matters;
  - assume there is only one way to achieve objectives;
  - abdicate responsibility;
  - check inputs rather than outputs; or
  - concentrate on failure and ignore success.

In other words, the client should hand the responsibility for service delivery to the contractor with appropriate briefing and training. Following the tender evaluation process, the client should assume that the contractor can deliver the service but will be aware of potential weaknesses that need early monitoring and closer management.

The client should not fear losing control or being let down. Contract management is the means of staying aware and in control without duplication of effort or confusion and possible conflict of roles.

❏ The interested parties

The two parties to the housing management contract are the client and the contractor. This will involve both officers and councillors on the client side and will involve officers and councillors on the contractor side if it is a DSO service provider.

Tenants and leaseholders as customers are the other key stakeholders. Their partnership involvement is discussed in the next section and elsewhere in this Guide.

Other interested parties that need to be taken account of in contract management include:

- Department of the Environment, particularly under the Local Government Acts 1988 and 1992 if the contractor is a DSO, but also in terms of performance generally;

- District Auditor with responsibility for ensuring proper procedure and value for money in the award of the contract and in respect of its monitoring and enforcement;

- internal auditor with responsibility for ensuring probity and the effectiveness of client procedures; and

- other contractors providing housing maintenance and estate services who may become part of a three-way relationship of contractor, client-agent and client as a result of the separation of client and contractor for housing management.

Housing management contract monitoring procedures and objectives need to be tested against the expectations, rights and responsibilities of all interested parties.

❏ A partnership involving customers, client and contractor

Effective contract management for housing services depends on a three-way working partnership between the client, the contractor and their shared customers. This does not, however, in any way undermine a contractual relationship or imply a legal partnership.

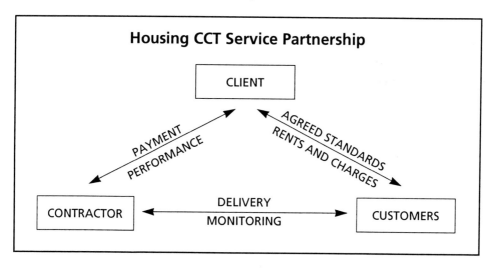

This is a new service relationship for all the parties and primary responsibility for making it work effectively rests with the client. Each of the three parties needs a defined role and structured input to the partnership. This means that, regardless of whether the service is won in-house or not, customers need to be able to comment on the service to the client without feeling that the client and contractor are one and the same thing. To serve the interests of customers, the client and contractor should work co-operatively but with a formal and visible separation of roles.

The formality of the separation of roles is easier to achieve and make visible if the housing management contract is awarded to an external organisation. However, in this situation it is perhaps harder to establish effective co-operation. The adversarial approach to contracting out, particularly under Government compulsion, has generated client mistrust of private sector bidders. However, there is little or no evidence that such bidders are less willing than a DSO to work in partnership with the client and customers. Indeed, the greater fear for customers might be that the lack of a formal contractual relationship between the client and a DSO will blur that role distinction and once again marginalise customer input to service monitoring and improvement.

Customers of housing management services have had their expectations raised through CCT. First, the service specification may be based on standards that were previously only aspired to or met to a greater or lesser frequency. They will expect the chosen contractor to deliver the specified services consistently. Second, customers may have influenced specified service levels and the choice of contractor. Those who want to maintain and develop that influence will look for a real and formalised role in monitoring service standards.

Customers will expect the contractor to perform to its tender submission promises whoever it turns out to be. They will also expect the standard of service to support the choice of contractor made by the client.

CHAPTER 2

PRE-CONTRACT ACTIVITIES

❑ Preparation

Between the announcement of the housing management contract and its commencement there is a period of some weeks (minimum 30 days, maximum 120 days, S.I. 1995 No.1336) when the formal working relationship between the client and contractor can be established. Proper use of this period is crucial to the initial success and long-term credibility of the housing management contract. A great deal of work may have already gone into planning for implementation. However, in the absence of certainty as to the identity of the contractor, the vital element of joint planning is likely to have been missing.

The experience of the voluntary delegations and competitive tendering of housing management is that it is a new experience for both the client and the contractor. This is equally true for a DSO contractor which will be familiar with the services and operational procedures but will not have experience of delivering these within a fee-based trading account and against a specification, customer monitoring and client management.

Regardless of the outcome of the tendering exercise, successful implementation of the contract is likely to depend on the following pre-contract activities.

❑ Approval of operational plans and procedures

The instructions to tenderers will probably have required submission of an operational plan. This is subject to client approval and provides an early opportunity for discussion of the realities of working as client and contractor towards a common goal of specified customer service. Method statements may also have been required and will be subject to client approval before they form the basis of agreed procedures.

These documents were required by the client and written by the contractor primarily with a view to tender evaluation. The competition over, both parties can revisit them as working documents which will be the basis of an agreed approach to service delivery and constructive joint working. Reaching such agreement will quite properly involve a degree of negotiation but, in case of doubt or disagreement, is governed by the written terms of the contract which should not be subject to negotiation at this stage.

❏ Training by the client

It is appropriate for the client to provide training for contractor staff where there is unfamiliarity with client policy and systems. Although particularly relevant to an external contractor bringing in new management, it may also be appropriate to provide initial training for DSO staff. Any expense should be charged to client budgets. The training programme is likely to continue into the early stages of the housing management contract and may recur periodically.

Some housing management contracts make it a requirement that contractor staff be released for set periods at set frequencies for training by the client. This is particularly relevant to authorities which are required by legislation to let multiple contracts and who may consequently have more than one contractor organisation. In these circumstances, mandatory training via the client on customer care or quality assurance can involve the sharing of experience and the joint development of skills.

❏ Joint review of performance indicators

The service specification will have set the standards and targets and described the required outcomes. It may also have listed the performance indicators by which these standards, targets and outcomes will be assessed. If these have been successfully piloted with a DSO which has subsequently been awarded the housing management contract then there may be need only for a cursory review and confirmation of joint understanding.

To a greater or lesser extent, however, there is a need for early and detailed discussion of what the standards, targets and outcomes mean in practice and which indicators will be used to assess performance. This should cover:

- basis of calculations, e.g. rent target;
- definition of terms, e.g. 'gross debit', 'relet void';
- division of responsibility between client, housing management contractor and third party contractors, particularly where there is joint input to achieving a target, e.g. voids; and
- source of performance information and responsibility for its retrieval and presentation, i.e. client or contractor.

This will be the first opportunity for the two parties to a housing management contract to discuss performance and to make the client's documentation fully workable as a basis for partnership and customer service. It is not, however, an opportunity to rewrite the contract by changing the scope of the services or the level of performance expectation.

❑ Liaison and meeting arrangements

The framework for liaison and meeting arrangements will be in the conditions of contract but will have been drafted to apply in the circumstances of any tendering outcome. The tendering outcome known, it is possible for the parties to sit down together, discuss reality and pool ideas. The result must satisfy the client and the contract conditions but is likely to be a development and improvement on the original arrangements devised in isolation.

The arrangements to be established should cover:

- frequency of meetings;
- types of meeting, their purpose and who should attend; and
- day-to-day liaison for advice and information, including named contacts for guidance on council systems, procedures and policies.

Liaison between the client and contractor will also be based on a certain amount of standard paperwork. It is very important that the client and contractor understand the purpose of standard forms and that appropriate officers of the council appreciate their importance and relative urgency. Otherwise, failures by the contractor to meet targets might be justified by inadequate briefing or action request forms being delayed with the authority's legal services or financial services.

❑ Client information requirements

Typically, the client will have thought it wanted to know **everything** about the operations of the housing management contractor. This is an entirely understandable product of fear of losing control of the service delivery and not knowing to whom one is losing control. Meeting the successful contractor, whoever it is, should allay much of the concern and allow consideration of the real need for information on operational matters.

Any prescribed information requirement should be limited to that which is:

- **relevant** to the client's retained responsibility; and
- **manageable** in scale and frequency to allow client consideration and consequent action.

Much of the contract management information will be readily available to both the client and the contractor through shared access to information technology (IT) systems. There will, however, be events, actions and progress reports for which the client is reliant on the contractor for information. The length of the list of such information will depend on the scope of the contract and extent of IT management applications but is illustrated overleaf.

Pre-contract discussions with the housing management contractor can establish **what** information is to be provided, **why** it is required, **when** it is needed and **how** it will be produced. This may result in an early clarification of the contract by formal agreement and side letter. It will certainly not be the last. Client information requirements will develop and be refined throughout the first year of the contract at least.

❑ Contractor information requirements

The housing management contractor's operations will depend on both ad hoc and regular information from the client. For example, it will need to know about key events that may be outside its direct responsibilities, such as house or flat sales and allocation decisions, and it will need up-to-date notification of budgets and policies and associated changes in these. Early discussion of what those requirements are and how they will be met will help to ensure the successful implementation of the contract and will reduce work and misunderstanding later. Information reasonably required by the housing management contractor from any part of the authority is a client responsibility. If that information is inaccurate, inadequate or inappropriately provided, it could give the housing management contractor a legitimate excuse for failure to perform.

Illustration of client information to be provided by the contractor

Events
- for immediate notification:
  - fire, civil disturbance or other event likely to promote councillor enquiries or media attention;
  - squatting; and
  - litigation.

- for periodic notification (weekly, monthly or quarterly, etc.):
  - number and category of customer complaints;
  - right to repair applications; and
  - casework numbers, i.e. nuisance, harassment, management transfer, unauthorised occupation, succession, assignment, mutual exchange, breach of tenancy conditions.

Actions
- compliance with procedures, e.g. types of arrears action within timescales and monetary value limits;
- accompanied viewings by number and percentage of lettings;
- service contract enforcement activity, e.g. notices served;
- meetings with service contractors evidenced by minutes and performance reports;
- pre-inspections of repairs;
- post inspections of repair works and consequent actions;
- repair satisfaction slips by number sent, response and consequent actions;
- achievement of standards and targets on home visits, correspondence, site inspections, welfare benefit, promotion;
- meetings with residents' associations evidenced by minutes, notes of walkabouts and schedules of actions;
- tenancy verifications by number and outcome; and
- exceptions reports or permitted action taken outside normal policy.

Progress
- expenditure commitments on client budgets;
- scheme progress and exception reporting on major works and planned maintenance;
- action and outcome against action plans to improve service contractor performance;
- actions and outcomes on all casework or by exception reporting according to timescale; and
- service development initiatives.

❑ Structures for councillor and customer input

The authority's councillors and customers will have been involved in the CCT process through to consultation on the identity of the preferred contractor and award of contract. The structures put in place for this will probably form the basis of a continuing involvement in managing the contract. This is discussed in more detail in the next chapter. However, the structures need to be formally established in the pre-contract period and both councillors and customer representatives are likely to need induction training for their roles. The key issues for consideration at this stage and which are referred to in the next chapter are:

- Government guidance and expectations on councillor and customer involvement;
- roles and responsibilities of councillors as ward representatives and collectively as a client committee or contractor board; and
- levels of continuing customer interest and structures for their input to committee decisions and delegated officer decisions.

❑ Service level agreements

Service level agreements (SLAs) are an important part of a local authority's corporate competition strategy. This large subject is outside the scope of this Guide but is covered by the Audit Commission publications *Behind Closed Doors: The Revolution in Central Support Services* 1994 and *Opening the Doors* 1995 and by the AMA publication *Service Level Agreements: Agreeing on Quality* 1991.

Under housing management CCT contracts the client is likely to be the purchaser (client) under any SLA for central support and specialist services, such as:

- information technology (IT) support;
- legal services;
- creditors and debtors systems; and
- other specialist services, e.g. building surveyor, environmental health, valuation.

However, under some housing management contracts the **contractor** is the purchaser of, for example, legal services either as client-agent using a client budget, or directly using contractor fee income to pay for the services.

The housing management contractor will depend on the effective delivery of these services for its own performance. It may also depend for its own operational effectiveness on the performance of direct housing services, falling outside the contract, such as:

- housing allocations; and

- housing benefit.

For any services that the contractor relies on but does not control, it is appropriate for the client to give assurances on performance. These assurances take the form of a SLA between the client and the contractor. The arrangements can be kept fairly simple but as a minimum, the contractor should know what to expect in terms of quality, quantity and timing. For example, in respect of:

- Allocations
    i) an allocation will be made and notified to the prospective tenant within x working days of the contractor providing a date for letting or within x days of a refusal, as appropriate;
    ii) the contractor will be notified of an allocation on the day it is made by copy of the offer letter; and
    iii) each allocation will be in accordance with household needs and stated preferences as provided for under council policy.

- Creditors
    i) invoices passed by the contractor for payments to third party service contractors will be either paid within x working days or referred back to the contractor for further work or consideration within x working days; and
    ii) notification of payments made will be posted to the relevant budget on the same day that the cheque is despatched.

The purpose of such a SLA is to recognise formally the relevance of the performance of other providers in monitoring the housing management contract. This may provide a basis for occasional justification of underperformance by the contractor; but it also maintains the focus on contractor performance when the SLA is being complied with. This balance is illustrated by the following extract from a legal services SLA.

London Borough of Richmond upon Thames

Extract from the Legal Services SLA for Housing Management CCT

Service	Housing management contractor obligations	Legal services obligations
Housing repossessions and rent arrears recovery	To provide clear and precise instructions, and any further information or details within 10 working days of request.	To acknowledge instructions within five working days of receipt, and respond with advice within 10 working days and/or to secure Court Hearing date within 40 working days of instructions being received or such further information having been provided.

Notes

It is noted and agreed that the setting or obtaining of Court dates is variable and inconsistent between Courts. It is not under the control of Legal Services. Due account of any such difficulties in failing to meet the general timescales will be made by the Housing Client Service.

If SLAs are not established by the tender documents, then they can be agreed prior to commencement of the contract. However, the client remains in a strong position in any negotiation of that agreement as by submitting a tender the contractor becomes bound by the specified performance level and the documentation pertaining at that time.

❑ Handover arrangements

Formal handover only applies if the contract goes to a new external housing management contractor. Preceding parts of this chapter form a part of that process. There are many other aspects, such as staff transfer under TUPE, lease arrangements for premises, equipment inventories and data transfer and access arrangements, but these are outside the remit of this Guide.

Nevertheless, for the purposes of contract management, an important handover of responsibility takes place for both a DSO and external contractor. Full client responsibility for contract management commences when the formal delegation of responsibility for delivery of the specified service occurs. The client will need to have developed and tested its own systems, structures and procedures by this date. This is done most effectively during a pre-tender 'dummy run' when both client and DSO can test all aspects of their prospective new relationship. If there is no time for a 'dummy run', a 'bedding in' period for both parties could be agreed covering the first three to six months of the contract.

Pre-contract planning in Dartford

DARTHOMES, the housing service of Dartford Borough Council, was transferred to the Hyde Housing Group by competitive tendering and voluntary delegation. Detailed joint planning for the transfer could only begin once the identity of the successful tenderer was known. This left just over three months to effect all the contract implementation arrangements. Even with rigorous project management on both sides it took all of that time to ensure successful implementation.

Both Dartford Council and Hyde had complementary action plans and met together regularly to ensure shared progress. Dartford Council used a specifically appointed project manager to drive through a 20 page action plan in a standard format, as follows:

Objectives	Tasks	Start date	People/depts involved	Accountable lead officer	Completion date

The objectives were broken down into a number of detailed tasks for each of which there was an assigned staff resource to perform the task and an accountable lead officer. The objectives were categorised under headings:

- **Operational** e.g. staff transfer;
  accommodation arrangements;
  monitoring and liaison;
  IT and management systems; and
  file and data transfer.

- **Financial** e.g. payment mechanism;
  budgetary control;
  invoice certification;
  VAT; and
  sundry cash collection arrangements.

- **Corporate** e.g. committee structure;
  resident involvement;
  disengagement from central services; and
  service level agreements.

CHAPTER 3

CONTRACT MONITORING

❏ Watchdog or bloodhound?

Part of the client role is similar to that of a watchdog, alert to the first signs that something is amiss. However, with the political sensitivity of housing management CCT, the client role can tend initially to be more that of a bloodhound on the basis of presumed wrongdoing that has to be 'sniffed out'.

In reality, a successful housing management contract will depend on the partnership approach outlined in Chapter 1. For the client to meet its responsibility without undermining that partnership, it will need to develop effective watchdog systems. The conditions of contract will probably contain provisions to support the bloodhound approach and it may become appropriate to use them. However, by this stage the partnership will have temporarily or permanently broken down, both parties to the contract may be partly to blame and the customers are the losers.

❏ A honeymoon period?

A 'honeymoon' (no default) period, when performance below standard is tolerated for a specified time, is sometimes used as an acknowledgement that a contractor cannot achieve the full contract standard from day one. The decision as to whether to allow such a period should depend on the nature and demands of the contract rather than the identity of the contractor. If there is to be a 'no default' period, the following should apply:

- the honeymoon relates only to the default procedure and not to the rigour of the monitoring;

- the length of the period should be determined in advance and communicated to the housing management contractor in writing – it should not be too long (perhaps two or three months with a maximum of six months), and might involve the phased introduction of the default procedure for an increasing number of performance areas;

- the client should consider both customer feedback and council priorities in determining whether certain performance areas are too important to fall within the 'no default' arrangement, e.g. office opening, courtesy to customers, rent income;

- for some performance areas it may be appropriate to relax rather than withdraw the default procedure during this initial period – this should be clearly set out in the notification to the housing management contractor, e.g. default at x + y weeks void rather than at x; and

- future working relations would be assisted if an informal record is kept of any defaults that would have applied which can then be discussed prior to the end of the 'no default' period.

The 'honeymoon period' for East Hertfordshire District Council

In East Hertfordshire there was a formal three-month relaxation of some specified requirements as the contractors were required to find their own accommodation in this period. A further three months was allowed for both the client and the contractors to fully establish their separate and joint operational methods. This mutually accommodating but businesslike approach was intended as the basis for a jointly understood and constructive relationship on service performance monitoring.

❏ Performance standards, targets and indicators

The contract is based on the expected achievement of the service standards described in the specification. These will include quantifiable standards such as frequencies of activity and timescales for action. They will also include qualitative standards for those actions and for the housing management contractor's approach and service reception environment.

For performance monitoring purposes, many of the standards will need to be translated into targets for sustained achievement or achievement at a certain date. As an example, the standard may be for answering the telephone within three rings and the target may be 85% compliance with the standard. Other examples of standards are that rent income be maximised and void periods be minimised. The targets for these may be 99% of debit and six weeks respectively in year one but with an agreed mechanism for revision of targets (upwards or downwards) in subsequent years of the contract.

Monitoring the achievement of **standards** and **targets** is based on **performance indicators**. For rent collection and voids the performance indicators are likely to be existing management system reports. Other objectively quantifiable indicators will be the output of processed performance data. However, the client will also need to devise indicators based on subjective judgement. Examples of service to which this will apply are complaints handling and professional judgements on casework. Subject to the provisions of the contract documentation, it is appropriate for the client to record such judgements as performance indicators both on a sample basis and in response to formal customer complaint. As subjective judgements, they are particularly susceptible to contractor challenge which underlies the need for the pre-contract joint review of performance indicators outlined in Chapter 2.

Example: indicators for subjective issues

Some clients propose to monitor the quality of correspondence sent by the contractor to customers. This is necessarily a somewhat subjective assessment but the client may quite reasonably see it as an important test of the quality of the service for which it remains accountable. The contractor would have to be advised of the indicators to be used which might include:

- correct and plain English;
- reader-friendly layout;
- absence of typographical error;
- factual accuracy; and
- helpfulness and adequacy of response.

Contract management derives its information in support of action from performance indicators. It is likely that the client and contractor will, for their own management purposes, use some common performance indicators and some that are specific to their needs.

Performance monitoring meetings between the client and contractor will probably be based on a wider set of performance indicators than would be appropriate to meetings involving customers although the client may wish to summarise the service implications of the wider set of indicators in order to receive customer reaction.

❑ Use of information technology

Information technology (IT) plays an increasingly important role in the delivery of responsive housing services and CCT has focused attention on its importance for the competitive efficiency of the contractor and the contract management responsibilities of the client. This is a large and important subject in itself which is given thorough coverage in the Association of District Councils and Chartered Institute of Housing guidance manual on *Competition and Local Authority Housing Services,* Module 6.

Key issues of concern for the client are:

- contractor system compatibility and interfaces with client systems, such as housing benefit and accounting;
- data ownership, maintenance and confidentiality;
- access to contractor performance information; and
- access to stock and tenancy data for meeting strategic and statutory housing responsibilities.

These and other concerns about CCT for both housing management and IT services are important considerations in drawing up the tender documentation. This is subject to Government *Guidance on Anti-competitive Behaviour* which states that, other than in exceptional circumstances, authorities may not require the use of their own IT systems under CCT. However, it has become apparent during the first round of CCT tendering that the successful housing management contractor is likely to use the client's information technology (IT) systems. In the event that this is not the case, specific contractual requirements for client approval, for system compatibility, interface and access and for data transfer, security, maintenance and disaster recovery should ensure a similar outcome in practice. In either case, the client would only give an external contractor access to data having ensured that it will be handled within the terms of registration under the Data Protection Act 1984 and the obligations of the Computer Misuse Act 1990.

Authorities have tended to offer the use of their own IT systems free of charge to the contractor. This has the advantages of encouraging their planned use by the tenderers, ensuring no increased cost for IT to the Housing Revenue Account (HRA) and avoiding a need for the DSO to make a return on IT assets. It also places the IT costs within the HRA client budget and makes the housing client responsible for maintaining IT services to the contractor. This should be subject to a service level agreement (SLA) between the client and contractor covering the level, frequency and response times of IT support, operational and development services. It may also be appropriate for the client at its own expense to provide introductory and refresher training to the contractor on use of the IT systems.

For contract monitoring and management the client will need management and financial information, performance monitoring information and the ability to calculate fee payments:

- **management and financial information** – the client needs to be able to identify early warnings and trends in demand and expenditure in order to monitor current budgets and make future spending plans;

- **performance information** – the client needs to be able to monitor progress and variance against the targets set for the contractor; and

- **fee-related information** – the system must be capable of providing the level of detail necessary to match the arrangements in the pricing schedule and to justify variations, incentive payments and liquidated damages.

Some authorities have introduced IT contract management applications for services other than housing management. These services, such as leisure management, are generally more input based and may have a large number of identifiable service sites. It is therefore possible to have an IT system which generates contractor defaults and payments based on downloaded inspection and cash receipting data. Housing management services, which are not so input driven, do not readily lend themselves to such an IT application.

The particular usefulness of IT for contract management in housing services is in its shared client and contractor on-line and report access to service performance indicators. The client will, however, need systems for validating the data by sample checking and for identifying trends and performance against standards and targets.

❑ When and how much to monitor

Monitoring should not become an industry and an end in itself. The specification describes the required service outcomes and the resource inputs, administrative processes and specific outputs that are essential to the delivery of those outcomes. In the same way, monitoring should focus on outcomes and limit the detail to that required to help to assess them. Nor should it be assumed that meeting the performance indicators necessarily adds up to a complete delivery of the required service outcomes. No amount of indicators can assess how the service is experienced by customers and over concentration on the detail of individual measures may result in the client losing sight of the overall picture.

Heavily input- and process-based specifications are a product of fear about what the then unknown successful housing management contractor might try and get away with. The danger is that such specifications would need a large monitoring team at a disproportionately high cost to the client and which consequently increases tenants' rent levels. Furthermore, in this situation the housing management contractor could be bogged down with responding to the minutiae of such monitoring. Worse still, the housing management contractor might reasonably claim that if it provides the required inputs and exactly follows client-prescribed procedures, it cannot be held responsible for deficiencies in the actual service outcomes.

As noted above, the pre-contract period provides an opportunity to discuss and establish the monitoring framework with the housing management contractor. The client may wish to retain some surprises (e.g. telephone response monitoring, spot checks and customer exit surveys) but it is generally sensible for both parties to understand the basis of the monitoring and their respective responsibilities for providing performance information.

It is also helpful to all concerned if monitoring proposals are discussed at the earliest possible stage with some other interested parties:

- **internal audit** will be the responsibility of the authority's head of finance and will have experience of establishing appropriate segregation of duties, systems, audit trails and cross checks. One client to a voluntary delegation of housing management said that internal audit 'practically lived in the department' for the first three months but that the result was very helpful in constructing the monitoring arrangements;

- **District Audit** will at some stage validate the approach. Experience in at least one authority suggests that the District Auditor may be unfamiliar with the nature of a housing management contract and, if poorly briefed by the client, could require far greater monitoring in pursuit of an unattainable and unnecessary (or uneconomic) level of certainty of contractor input; and

- **other contractors** providing repairs and estate services may offer to assist in the provision of monitoring information in order to contribute positively to new working arrangements following contract commencement. (However, they cannot be forced to do this unless such requirements are within their contract conditions.)

The techniques and frequencies of monitoring and control will depend on the scope of the contract and the corporate culture. An illustration is given overleaf from East Hertfordshire District Council which let two area-based contracts by competitive tendering and voluntary delegation to Anglia Housing Association Group and Network Housing Association.

❑ The monitoring role of customers

Section 10 of the Local Government Act 1992 requires that throughout the period of the contract with a DSO or external contractor:
- a copy of the specification and a summary of the specification is made available by the local authority for public inspection; and
- publicity is given, sufficient to draw this arrangement to the attention of members of the public who may be interested.

Section 27A of the Housing Act 1985 (as amended by the Leasehold Reform, Housing and Urban Development Act 1993) requires that throughout the period of a management agreement the local authority:
- makes suitable arrangements for affected tenants to make their views known on standards of service; and
- considers any such representations made prior to a decision with respect to enforcement action under the agreement.

It should be noted that the 1985 Act does not apply in Scotland (although guidance is given in Scottish Office Circular 20/1995) and that the Section is specific to a management agreement and would not in strict legal terms, therefore, cover a DSO. However, for the purposes of guidance under the 1985 Act on *Tenant Involvement in Housing Management* [1994] the Department of the Environment defines management agreement as including a service level agreement with a DSO. The Department, therefore, regards the legislative position as covering tenant and leaseholder involvement in the monitoring of all housing management contracts and it expects authorities to exceed the minimum statutory requirement. In practice, all authorities should plan for and implement comparable customer involvement for external contracts and DSO service level agreements. Guidance on this is available from both the Tenant Participation Advisory Service (TPAS) and the Priority Estates Project (PEP). Detailed advice is also given in Module 8 of the Association of District Councils and Chartered Institute of Housing guidance manual on *Competition and Local Authority Housing Services*.

The starting point for individual customer involvement and meeting the requirements of the 1992 Act is the provision of information on contract standards in a user-friendly summary form. A number of authorities have attempted this as part of the consultation on the specification and with some success. One model for taking this forward to the monitoring stage is being

East Hertfordshire District Council

Monitoring of Repairs, Maintenance and Capital Works

Control objective:

To ensure that the Council's housing stock is maintained to an acceptable standard.

	Control objective	Frequency of monitoring
1.	Repairs and maintenance budgets and capital works are approved by the Council	– annual (subject to periodic review in consultation with housing contractor)
2.	Contractor is notified of the Council's repairs and maintenance policy and approved capital programme	– as above
3.	Repair and maintenance and capital works procedures are documented in the service delivery statement and this has been approved by the Supervising Officer	– annual, provided by housing contractor prior to year commencement
4.	The Supervising Officer approves the contractor's plans and cash flows to achieve the above strategies	– as above
5.	Changes to the contractor's profiles of expenditure to be approved by the Supervising Officer	– four weekly meeting with contractor
6.	Supervising Officer monitors progress against the approved expenditure profiles	– four weekly meeting with contractor
7.	The Supervising Officer reports to Committee on progress against achieving the approved budgets	– quarterly
8.	Systematic inspection of works by client to ensure compliance with service delivery statement including both revenue and capital works:	– weekly programme of site visits
	• confirmation that all transactions are supported by legitimate invoices;	– as received
	• a 5% detailed inspection of individual transactions to confirm that:	
	– appropriate budgets exist for the expenditure;	
	– Financial Regulations and Standing Orders have been complied with;	on-going random selection and scrutiny of documentation and works on site; and periodic systems audit
	– appropriate systems of internal control are in place;	
	– appropriate methods of placement of work have been utilised;	

Control objective	Frequency of monitoring
– payments made to building contractors have been correctly authorised, are valid and correct and accounted for correctly; – the transaction does not represent a duplicate payment; – services and works have been received; and – that value for money has been achieved;	on-going random selection and scrutiny of documentation and works on site; and periodic systems audit
• sample testing to confirm that work being placed is necessary and placed in appropriate fashion	– detailed investigation of 20 jobs per housing contractor per annum (and more if initial investigations give cause for concern)

9. Contractor to provide:

– a progress statement on repairs and maintenance and capital works including actual/committed expenditure against the allocated budget (in accordance with the budget profiles and cash flows in the housing contractor's service plan);	– four weekly meeting with contractor
– evidence of x% pre-inspections including numbers and percentages achieved;	– as above
– evidence of 10% post inspections of all work exceeding £250 including numbers and percentages achieved;	– as above
– results of 20% tenants' customer satisfaction survey and action taken to improve satisfaction levels;	– as above
– number of responsive repairs ordered and achievement against priority times;	– as above
– progress against special category works, servicing and maintenance;	– as above
– progress against planned and cyclical repair, maintenance and servicing programmes;	– as above
– progress against special category works, servicing and maintenance;	– as above
– details of remedial works; and	– as above
– details of tenants' complaints received and actions taken	– as above

10. Payment controls — – as detailed in specific monitoring schedule for all payments

11. Contractor to provide the Supervising Officer with the results of the 10% survey of Council stock as previously agreed — – half yearly

The results of the survey to be incorporated into future budgetary decisions by the Council — – annually developed by Oxford City Council. The authority has drafted a number of service guarantees covering:

- repairs and service contracts;
- rent services;
- lettings;
- tenancy services;
- estate management;
- consultation; and
- right to buy.

Each of these service guarantees to customers extracts the service standards from the specification and sets out what will be done, by when and how this will happen and/or be checked, as illustrated below.

In Oxford, these service guarantees are further summarised and the main points are to be distributed to all tenants. The full guarantees are available to

Oxford City Council

Extract from the Repairs and Service Contracts Customer Guarantee

IF	WE WILL ...	WHEN	HOW/CHECKS
you report a repair to us which needs inspecting before any work is ordered	(a) tell you in writing, when your repair will be inspected (b) inspect it to check exactly what work is needed and whether it is our responsibility	within 10 days of you reporting your repair to us	you will be offered a morning or afternoon appointment for a particular date
your repair is one that needs to be done by a specialist contractor	keep you up to date on what is happening and how long it is likely to take	at all times	
you're not satisfied with the quality of a repair carried out at your home	either visit you to check for ourselves what needs to be done or call the contractor back	within one working day of you telling us that there is a problem	all repairs notifications will have a customer satisfaction slip for you to fill in and return to us
there's a delay in doing your repair	(a) 'chase' the repair on your behalf	either as part of a regular weekly chase of all overdue repairs or within one working day of it being over-due, if you ask us	
	(b) where we have been told of a delay by one of our contractors we will pass this information on to you	within one working day of being told about the delay by our contractor	

those who request them. In this way they provide for an informed input by tenants both individually as consumers and collectively as representatives on panels or local boards.

Other means of encouraging and obtaining individual customer feedback on contractor performance are referred to in Module 8 of the ADC/CIH *Competition and Local Authority Housing Services* manual including:

- attitude surveys;
- complaints procedure;
- comments slips; and
- periodic questionnaires.

These provide direct and cost-effective monitoring information which will form a picture of whether a contract is going well or not. It may also help to pinpoint deficiencies for remedial action. However, apart from the most obvious of failures that can be remedied in response to a complaint (e.g. unwashed stairs), the monitoring by customers of both contractor performance and client response will necessitate their formal and collective involvement.

A number of models are being developed by TPAS, PEP and individual authorities for collective and representative customer involvement to suit a variety of local circumstances. These models range from unelected customer panels, through registered tenant/leaseholder associations to hierarchical arrangements of estate-based, area-based and borough-wide organisations feeding into monitoring and service development decision making by the council. Emerging as a fairly common feature is a periodic meeting with customers, the client and the contractor. One of the most tried and tested of these models is in the London Borough of Brent where a service customer holds the chair of each of the Area Boards which monitors performance and the consequent actions of both the contractor and the commissioning client.

❑ The monitoring role of councillors

Section 7(8) of the 1988 Act requires that in carrying out work an authority must comply with the detailed specification. An authority should require the same standards of performance from a successful in-house team as would have been required from an external contractor and monitor the performance of the work on that basis. The Secretary of State is of the view that if the work is to be performed by the in-house team an authority can best demonstrate that it is complying with this condition by preparing reports to the appropriate committee on a regular basis assessing the performance of the Direct Services Organisation against the specification.

Guidance on the Conduct of Compulsory Competitive Tendering. Consultation Draft. Department of the Environment – October 1995

The objective of councillor involvement, on behalf of residents, is to secure best value for money in delivering local priorities and specified standards. In order to perform their monitoring function effectively, therefore, they will need to concentrate their attention on both:

- how the contractor is performing in delivering the services; and
- how the client is performing in improving, maintaining and developing the services.

This is an essential part of managing housing services through a client commissioner and a contractor provider. It should also clarify officer responsibilities and assist councillors in focusing on the accountable client or contractor officer. This is recognised within the approach to councillor monitoring adopted by the London Borough of Brent.

Councillor monitoring – London Borough of Brent

Councillor involvement in service monitoring takes place at two levels:

1. **The service committee** receives reports at each cycle on:
   - key performance indicators against targets for the service as a whole;
   - performance by individual housing management contractors;
   - actions taken by the client, the purposes, outcomes and proposals; and
   - a major area of service, e.g. voids, in accordance with a pre-timetabled cycle of reports covering current performance and proposals for improvements.

2. **A performance review committee** is responsible for the client methods and effectiveness across the range of contracted services and will periodically receive reports on a single service area, e.g. housing management, building cleaning, grounds maintenance.

   In Brent, the local monitoring of performance at area contract level is carried out by Area Boards of residents at which councillors can attend but do not have voting rights.

Having been used to a very direct influence over housing performance, councillors will have to learn to act as a client to a contracted service. If the contractor is a DSO there may be a corporate or housing DSO board made up of other councillors which is charged with responding to client committee concerns in addition to internal DSO concerns.

Councillors will also need to understand their relationship with the service at ward representative level. Customers, and councillors on their behalf, should be able to raise operational matters and formal complaints with the contractor verbally or in writing. However, they will need to direct any policy issues or concerns about the specification to the client. In the anticipated spirit of partnership these distinctions can quite reasonably be dispensed with in much of the day-to-day common search for service solutions. However, the distinctions must underpin the ward councillor role, the complaints procedure and any dispute over the specified service standard.

❑ Quality assurance systems

Some contracts for local authority services are now being evaluated partly on the basis of the quality assurance (QA) systems of the tenderers. The purpose of this is to establish a 'self-monitoring' basis to the contract where the contractor monitors its own performance on an ongoing basis. The client then has the option of conducting sample checks of the contractor's own QA system rather than the more staff-intensive checking of a large number of service outputs.

A number of the housing management contracts have required the contractor to operate a QA system but in most cases this appears to be part of a general test of quality rather than a means of reducing or focusing the client monitoring input. There is clearly greater scope for using contractor QA systems as a basis for 'self-monitoring' of consistency of standards and response. Accreditation under a recognised standard such as EN ISO 9000 would help in giving assurance of the housing management contractor's processes but is time consuming to attain and may be regarded as a diversion of effort by contractors.

Brent quality systems

In the London Borough of Brent, the contractor is required to demonstrate, at six-monthly intervals, progress towards the registration of its management system under EN ISO 9002 or equivalent. At tender stage the requirement is set out as follows:

- the contractor is required to offer a quality assured housing service to residents of the housing management area, and is required to design and provide services in accordance with the provisions of the contract with the Council;

- the contractor shall provide an annual Quality Plan detailing how quality services will be developed and delivered;

- the contractor will be required to define and document its policy and objectives for and commitment to quality. The contractor shall also carry out all the planned and systematic management actions necessary to provide adequate confidence that it will satisfy all the given requirements for quality provision. This shall include:

  (a) defining the responsibility, authority and interrelation of all personnel;
  (b) establishing, maintaining and implementing written procedures and systems;
  (c) identifying adequate trained staff to provide the performance information specified;
  (d) establishing and maintaining a documented quality system to ensure that the service conforms to all specified requirements;
  (e) establishing and maintaining procedures to control all documents and data to ensure that appropriate documents are available at the location where the operation is performed and that obsolete documents are removed;
  (f) ensuring that other contracted services conform to specified requirements;
  (g) establishing, documenting and maintaining procedures for ascertaining and correcting the cause of non-compliance with the service standards specific to prevent recurrence;
  (h) establishing and maintaining procedures for the identification, collection, storage, retrieval and maintenance of records/files; and
  (i) carrying out a comprehensive system of planned and documented internal quality audits, and implementing appropriate corrective action on any deficiencies found.

However, while a QA system may provide consistency of standards it does not set the quality of those standards against a specified client requirement. Performance monitoring against the specification and customer feedback will still be required although it may be possible for the client to concentrate more on the service outcomes and leave the checking of the inputs and processes to sample testing of the contractor's QA system.

The client should also consider a quality assurance system for its own processes. Client contract management responsibilities are to a large extent procedural and quality assurance of all aspects would benefit the customers and the contractor.

CHAPTER 4

CONTRACT ADMINISTRATION

❏ Need for a corporate approach

In taking action and making decisions on contract administration, the client is managing its relationship with the contractor and customers based on service performance and requirements and the terms of the contract. However, this takes place within a wider framework which will include some or all of the following:

- council financial regulations;
- statutory control of the contracting of and payment for public sector work;
- service level agreements (e.g. legal and financial services);
- third-party contracts (e.g. repairs); and
- client-agent responsibilities for support services externalised through CCT or voluntary tendering.

As more council services are subjected to competition, the framework becomes more complicated and in greater danger of fragmentation and internal conflict. Corporate CCT strategies which have emerged to manage this danger at tender stage, need to extend into support and direction for the contract administration functions. Otherwise, the client may be distracted by dealing with the 'corporate competition machinery'.

❏ Corrective action and default procedures

The principal client objective of contract management is to secure the specified service, at least to the contract standard and at the agreed price.

If the working relations between client and the housing management contractor are good, then this can be achieved through discussion and joint case reviews and site visits. However, serious and persistent service failures will require more formal use of the default provisions contained in the contract conditions. Such provisions will vary between contract documents but most are likely to apply equally to a DSO or external contractor.

Various models have been developed for taking escalating enforcement action against service contractors. The terminology varies but the principles remain the same:

- seek resolution at the first stage of client or direct customer involvement;
- minimise the bureaucracy;
- reflect the seriousness of the service failure in any action taken or documentation served;
- allow for discussions at each stage involving progressively more senior client management and more senior contractor representation if not already involved;
- relate any reduction in fee payment to the financial loss sustained by the client, by quantifying additional costs to the client, e.g. staff time, employment of consultants to investigate and/or rectify the situation. (This could allow for a small core of client staff to be augmented by additional personnel when necessary and at the contractor's expense.);
- avoid procedure-driven escalation of action which can lead to a premature threat of contract termination; and
- use the dispute resolution services of a third party in the form of an 'expert' or arbitrator. The Chartered Institute of Housing is in the process of establishing a specialist arbitration service to assist in such matters.

Applying these principles to a housing management contract, the procedure for corrective action is likely to include the following stages (although the terminology may vary):

- **informal resolution** of a customer complaint or client notification of service failure which may not require written record or further action;
- **programmed site visits** held jointly between the client, contractor and customers;
- **Compliance Notice** served by the client on the contractor and requiring rectification of a more serious or persistent service failure.

The Notice may be a written follow-up to a verbal instruction and will specify the required action and timescale. If the Notice is complied with, defaults or financial reductions may not be necessary. An illustration of a Compliance Notice is at Appendix A;

- **Warning Notice** notifying the contractor that it is in breach of the contract and advising of the actions and timescale necessary to avoid further action. A Warning Notice may follow a Compliance Notice or may be the first action if the service failure is sufficiently serious, e.g. failure to open the office, or unnotified overspend of a delegated budget. A record of delivery of all Warning Notices should be retained. An illustration of a Warning Notice is at Appendix B;

- **Default Notice** giving notification to the contractor of the nature and consequences of a service failure or accumulation of service failures. For some contracted services, e.g. building cleaning, with more visible input and output requirements, the Default Notice is often the first action to be taken by a client. However, for the more process- and outcome-based service requirements of housing management, it may be more appropriate for notification of default to accompany a Warning Notice or a given number of Compliance Notices. The format of such notification will, therefore, depend on the provisions in the conditions of contract and a standard illustration is not appropriate here.

Default Notices are usually related to reductions in fee payment. This can either be a direct relationship or based on a points system with thresholds that trigger financial reductions. In either case such reductions in fee must be in the form of liquidated damages and:
- the basis of the calculation of liquidated damages must have been set out in the tender documents; and
- fee reductions that do not represent a genuine reasonable pre-estimate of the cost that would be incurred by the client in rectifying the default may be deemed penalties and unenforceable in law.

An actual reduction in fee to the DSO or external contractor might be implemented in cases where warranted. However, should Default Notices arise, whether or not a fee reduction is made, a record of their number and financial value can serve as a basis for councillor monitoring of both contractor service provision and client contract management performance;

- **dispute resolution** by an expert or arbitrator, will result in a decision that is binding on both parties. The ADC/AMA *Model Form of Contract for Housing Management Services* uses the term 'expert'. In practice, disputes may well involve an arbitrator who will appoint an expert witness in disputes over matters of professional judgement (see reference to CIH Arbitration Service above);

- **Notice of Termination** is the final threat which may have been served prior to invoking a dispute resolution clause in the contract conditions. In these circumstances, both the client and contractor will need to consider how it came about and could have been avoided. It should be recognised that a contract with a DSO **can** be terminated. The 1992 Local Government Management Board *CCT Information Service – Survey Report* found that, of the 66 contracts that had been terminated for reasons other than by Government requirement following Section 14, 1988 Act notices, 29 had been held by DSOs that could not sustain the required service within their bid price.

❑ Variations and additional works

A housing management contract sets the scope and standard of service for three to five years. It will almost certainly provide for variations and additions so that the client can respond to changing circumstances and experience of the contract. However, other forms of Government regulation govern the extent to which the contract payment can be increased by variation or addition without further competition. (See CIH/ADC *Competition and Local Authority Housing Services* manual, Module 4 for detailed advice.)

Minor variations and additions should not present a problem. However, housing clients may already have experienced the restrictions on their ability to legitimately award new work under existing building maintenance contracts with a direct labour organisation without undertaking a further competitive tendering exercise. Similar restrictions apply to a housing management contract. For either a DSO or external contractor, the client will be constrained by the authority's financial regulations and standing orders relating to contracts and by the requirements of the District Auditor. However, even more stringent restrictions apply under the CCT legislation to a DSO carrying out a defined activity – see the Association of District Councils and Chartered Institute of Housing guidance manual *Competition and Local Authority Housing Services* Module 4.

There are no easy answers to this problem for either a defined or non-defined activity. A decision to delegate an additional service such as right to buy or homelessness administration to an existing contractor may make operational sense. However, in the light of the authority's duty to secure value for money in expending public funds, legal and (possibly) District Audit advice is needed if this is proposed to be done on a negotiated fee basis, rather than further competitive tendering.

Some clients have made provision for this in the tender by asking for a price for a service that may be delegated at a later stage. Detailed tender pricing schedules that include hourly or day rates for different grades of staff may also help to substantiate a fee for additional work. Ultimately, it will be a matter of judgement, first by the client but also by the statutory finance officer and possibly the District Auditor.

Example: pricing schedule for hourly/daily rates for staff

The tenderer shall enter the appropriate rates below for the categories of work described.

Work type/grade	Monday-Friday		Saturday		Sunday & Bank Holidays	
	Hourly £	Daily £	Hourly £	Daily £	Hourly £	Daily £
Clerical						
Technical						
Professional and managers						
Second tier contract management						
Contract manager						

Length of working day: _____ hours

Overtime rates applying to additional hours _____

CHAPTER 5

MANAGING THE CONTRACTUAL RELATIONSHIP

❏ The contractor as client-agent

Most housing management contracts will include delegated responsibility for managing services provided by a third party. With this comes the contractor responsibility of committing expenditure and possibly certifying payment against client budgets.

Some of this delegation will be relatively straightforward and will only need periodic monitoring of expenditure against budget, e.g. communal heating and landlord lighting.

Other delegations are more sensitive, particularly if they are made to an external contractor where the contract is the only formal means of control. The most obvious of these is responsibility for commissioning repairs and managing the associated budget. For this the client will be concerned about the following:

- **a demand-led service** will mean that expenditure will have seasonal and other variations which will complicate budget monitoring. The contractor should be made responsible for providing an anticipated profile of expenditure within the annual operational plan as a basis for monitoring;

- **contractor discretion** in applying council policy and responding to individual circumstances could lead to additional expenditure, for example in response to tenant complaint or to facilitate letting of void property. Contractor discretion should be limited to specified types of circumstance with a requirement that discretionary deviation from normal policy is recorded for client inspection (or pre-authorised over a specified level of expenditure);

- **quality and quantity of repairs** obtained within the budget will depend on professional judgement of the contractor in achieving the right repair in the circumstances and best value for money. This will partly be controlled by spot checking the contractor's inspection records, application of a schedule of rates contract and compliance with the council's financial regulations. Other client monitoring will involve year on year comparisons and discussion with the contractor of budget requirements, trends and any special circumstances that have applied; and

- **the client-agent role of the contractor** can blur lines of accountability if not carefully specified. The housing management contractor is accountable for its service responsibilities and cannot shift this onto a third-party contractor on the grounds of that third party's underperformance. If the housing management contractor is responsible for the repairs service through client-agent management of a third-party contractor, then the housing management contractor must have undertaken all of its responsibilities in relation to that client-agent role before formally seeking to absolve itself of responsibility for service deficiency. The client should normally look, in the first instance, to the housing management contractor until and unless it is notified and satisfied that this contractor has met its client-agent responsibilities.

Much the same concerns will apply to other budgeted services that are delegated to the contractor. These may include:

- grounds maintenance;
- building cleaning;
- mechanical and electrical maintenance; and
- other services, e.g. pest control, inspections, valuation.

❏ Multiple contracts

There is no evidence to date of authorities tendering contracts for individual functions (e.g. rents, repairs, caretaking) under CCT. Area-based generic contracts are the preferred approach. However, some authorities are required under the CCT legislation to tender more than one area-based housing management contract because of the size of their stock.

If the same contractor wins all the contracts, this may simplify contract management. If contracts are awarded in different years it will also help if the successful contractor is already 'on site'.

Simplicity may not always provide the best results, however, and there are possible advantages in having different contractors generating new ideas and a degree of performance competition. The client will want to harness these energies but will also need to avoid fragmentation of the service. In particular, the client will need to guard against contractor 'buck-passing' and resistance to accepting particular tenants by transfer or allocation.

Safeguards can be provided within the contract by requiring regular liaison and a structured sharing of information between contractors. A common IT system and database will assist in this, although ability to alter data and update action reports will need to be regulated via controls on access and tamper-proof audit trails between the contractors as well as between them and the client.

Where there is more than one contract, each should be separately monitored by the client and local customers. Where there is more than one contractor organisation each will be managed separately by the client. However, joint meetings of the client and all contractors, and possibly relevant service contractors, are recommended for the purposes of service planning and performance review. Management of such meetings will need a high level of client management skill and knowledge, including chairing, negotiating, and understanding contract legislation.

❑ A contractor in difficulties

The primary purpose of this Guide is to consider client responsibility for ensuring service delivery through an effectively managed contract. This could be jeopardised if the contractor runs into difficulties and increasingly concentrates on survival tactics or damage limitation; for example, putting staff resources only into activities that influence payments under the contract such as void control and rent collection.

In the adversarial approach to contracting noted in this Guide, there has been a tendency for authorities to see such difficulties as only the contractor's problem. Indeed, clients have sometimes taken comfort that this demonstrates that they secured the 'right' price, and are managing effectively.

It is certainly true that contracting services out passes responsibility for price to the contractor. However, the client is responsible for its tender evaluation decisions and is accountable to the tenants and leaseholders as end users. Primary responsibility for delivery of the service rests with the contractor but it is appropriate for the client to engage in positive dialogue if the contractor seeks assistance through review of the contract conditions and their application.

This is not to suggest that the contractor be absolved from its responsibilities in terms of 'under bidding' to win the contract. On the contrary, the objective is to sustain the contractor's input at an acceptable level. This is a sensitive area, however, and in particular, the client must be seen to be dealing properly with a DSO that fails to deliver the services within the bid price if it is not to breach the CCT legislation (see Module 4 of the ADC/CIH manual for further information).

Ultimately, the tests of reasonableness of action will include accountability to customers and demonstrable value for money in expenditure of public funds. On the basis of application of these tests, it may be appropriate to temporarily or permanently apply one or more options including the following:

- no defaults for a defined service area and period of time to allow for planned and agreed corrective action;

- contract variation to remove responsibility for a service presenting difficulties that can then be placed with another contractor;

- contract variation to provide additional work generating justifiable additional fee income and spreading costs; or

- meeting in part or in full a contractor claim against the client based on the argument that tender documents misled the contractor at tender stage or that circumstances have arisen that have a material effect but could not reasonably have been foreseen by either party. (In the case of a DSO, this will probably require third party substantiation.)

If the contractor fails to remain solvent or to deliver the specified service despite proper and reasonable client assistance then that is, of course, the contractor's responsibility and the contract may be terminated.

❑ What if the contractor fails?

The conditions of contract will provide for its termination in the event of serious breach of the requirements and terms. This covers a range of circumstances, including termination by the client on grounds of performance and the contractor being wound-up, being put into receivership or walking off site. Depending on these circumstances, the termination may be for the whole or part of the contract, leaving the client with the immediate need to make alternative arrangements to cover all or part of the services.

The conditions of contract should also provide for the additional costs of the alternative arrangements to be charged to the defaulting contractor.

If the failed contractor is a DSO, the failure will almost certainly be a result of being unable to sustain the service within the bid price. In such circumstances there will be sufficient notice and a direct local authority employment relationship with contractor staff which, together, should provide time for retendering and handover to the successful contractor. Nonetheless, in these unfortunate and unwanted circumstances, the client should be aware of the likely effects on service delivery, of staff disaffection and search for jobs elsewhere.

If a contract is terminated with an external contractor, the client can bring the service in-house during the period of retendering. A further Transfer of Undertakings (TUPE) may or may not apply depending on the details of the arrangement. However, it is probably that staff of the contractor will be willing to work for the local authority if the contractor is in financial difficulties.

As an alternative, the client may make an interim arrangement with another contractor. Again, the application of TUPE would depend on the details of that arrangement. In a multiple contract authority this arrangement might be with the service provider in another contract area or it may be that the authority will need to look to its neighbours or further afield. At the time of writing, it would appear that the DSO of another local authority might also be allowed to provide the services, subject to clarification of the Government's position on 'cross-border trading'.

Of course, insofar as the terminated contract relates to services that are not part of the relevant percentage (i.e. 95% for housing management) of the 'defined activity' (1988 Local Government Act) then the services can be brought in-house and do not have to be retendered.

The purpose of this Guide is to help the client to avoid these outcomes.

CHAPTER 6

CONCLUSION

❑ The client-contractor split

The legislatively enforced introduction of a client/contractor split in housing services has often brought uncertainty of roles, unproductive disruption to working practices and some animosity between the two staff groups. It could be argued that a split of responsibilities has always existed between making policy commitments and setting standards on the one hand and making management arrangements and deploying resources to meet them on the other. However, these roles have hitherto been carried out by the same group of councillors advised by the same group of officers. In other words, the same people are setting the standards, resourcing delivery and monitoring their own performance. To suggest this is unsatisfactory is not an argument for CCT but it does point to the positive aspects of a formal split between those accountable for a published level of service and those bound by an agreement that they have the resources to deliver that specified service level. These have come to be referred to under CCT as the client and contractor roles.

This Guide has argued the importance of what is generally termed the client role, regardless of whether the contract is won internally or externally, and has provided some of the principles of good practice for success in that role once the contract has been let.

❑ The client as manager

By tendering and entering into a contract the contractor has taken on management responsibility for all aspects of specified service delivery. This large management task should be made more straightforward by the existence of a specification but in other respects it remains a major challenge with a clear responsibility for consistent service delivery within a fee budget. At the same time, the client has taken on a new and probably unfamiliar management role with accountability for a service that has to be delivered through effective delegation to the contractor. This is also a challenging management task, despite a reduction in numbers of directly managed staff, and it may necessitate the development of new skills in addition to good practice guidance.

❑ Customer service

The overall conclusion that can be drawn from this Guide is that the interests of customers are best served if the client and contractor work constructively together. What is meant by working constructively is that the terms and service standards set out in the contract should not be undermined by a client and contractor relationship which is either too permissive or too adversarial. Customers may want to have a direct input to making that relationship effective or they may, quite reasonably want to leave it to officers who they pay for the service through their rents and service charges. In either case, they will want to know what service they should receive, who is accountable for it and what response they should get if they complain.

Appendix A

COMPLIANCE NOTICE
Serial No: 1132

To:

From:

Date:

You are hereby required to comply with the Conditions of Contract by supplying the services and carrying out the actions to the standard and timescale set out below. In the event that you fail to comply with this requirement, the Council shall be entitled to treat this as a breach of contract for the purposes of Condition 45*.

Compliance required:

Signed: _____
    Contract Monitoring Officer

*Note: Based on the provisions of Condition 45 Termination, Etc. in the ADC/AMA *Model Form of Contract for Housing Management Services.*

APPENDIX B

WARNING NOTICE
pursuant to Condition 45* of the
Contract for Housing Management Services Serial No: 019

To: The Contract Manager [   ] Housing Services

From: The Authorised Officer [   ] District Council

Date: [   ]

You are hereby advised that as of the above date you are in breach of contract on the grounds that the specified services have not been provided or have not been undertaken with due skill and care or have not been carried out adequately the particulars of which are set out at (1) below. The required rectification is set out at (2) below.

(1)   Particulars of breach of contract:

(2)   Required rectification:

You are further warned that in the event of the Council serving upon you a total number of either three (3) Warning Notices in any six month period or four (4) Warning Notices in any twelve month period, the Council shall be entitled (without prejudice to it) to exercise all or any of its rights under condition 45* and for the purposes of this Condition a 'six month period' or 'twelve month period' shall be taken as meaning in respect of any date the immediately preceding period of six months or twelve months respectively.

Signed: _____
        Chief Housing Officer for [   ] District Council

*Note: Based on the provisions of Condition 45 Termination, Etc. in the ADC/AMA *Model Form of Contract for Housing Management Services.*

APPENDIX C

❏ Glossary

Application	An information technology program or series of programs used to undertake a practical function.
Audit trail	An assessment procedure (which may be part of a computerised system) which shows who has done what and when in financial (and operational) terms. It can establish both compliance with procedure and probity.
Client-agent	Organisation with a contractual responsibility for managing a contract for supply of works or services on behalf of the housing management client.
Contract administration	Management of the practical details and formalities of the contractual relationship.
Contract monitoring	System(s) implemented by a local authority to record and act upon the performance of the contractor against the specified inputs, outputs, processes and targets.
Contract standard	The standard of service delivery and performance outcomes described by the contract documents.
Customer care	Ascertaining what a customer wants and needs and acting accordingly whilst respecting the customer as a valued purchaser of the service.
Downloaded inspection data	Information received from a computer network or individual (possibly handheld) computer in a form allowing interrogation.

EN ISO 9002	The international standard for quality systems where an organisation is offering a service to a published specification.
Indicator	Measure which can be evaluated to show whether an organisation is achieving its published or required performance standards.
Input	Specified input requirement such as office opening hours and numbers and expertise of people on duty.
Management agreement	An agreement by a local authority, in England or Wales, under Section 27 of the Housing Act 1985, by which another person or organisation exercises on its behalf some or all of the authority's housing management functions.
Multiple contract authorities	Local authorities that have been required by CCT legislation or have chosen to let more than one contract for the delivery of housing management services.
On-line access	Direct access to an information technology system in real time allowing data to be input and information to be extracted.
Operational plan	Annual plan by the contractor, subject to prior approval by the client, setting out resources and a timetable of action and target dates for delivery of the specified services.
Outcome	The result or effect of the delivery of a service as specified by the client and/or as experienced by the customer.
Output	Specified service event or product described in terms of quality and speed of response, e.g. customer correspondence, home visit, report.

Pre-contract

Period or activities undertaken after award of a contract but prior to the contract commencement date.

Process

Procedure or series of inputs and/or outputs leading to a required service outcome

Quality assurance system

The British Standards Institute defines a Quality System as "the organisational structure, responsibilities, procedures, processes and resources for implementing quality management". Assurance is the integration of all these elements to provide a 'fail-safe' mechanism and a regulatory operational framework.

Service level agreements (SLAs)

An agreement between two bodies or departments as to levels, frequencies and, where relevant, the charges for services that one relies on from the other in performing its own responsibilities.

Service plan

Approved account of the priorities, aims, performance objectives, resources and operational timetable for the delivery of a service.

Service site

Point of delivery e.g. area office from which the housing management service is delivered.

Target

Translation of standards into a definable measure of performance of our progress towards those standards.

TUPE

Transfer of Undertakings (Protection of Employment) Regulations 1981, these regulations derived from EU legislation carry the terms and conditions of employment of existing employees from the current employer to the new employer when services they provide are transferred as part of an undertaking.